The Little Book
Of
Magic Spells
For
Witches

ISBN-13: 978-1478381419

ISBN-10: 1478381418

DEDICATION

For all those people who love a little bit of magic in their lives.

CONTENTS

Magic, the very word itself has fascinated and horrified humanity for thousands of years.

Some consider it the purest and most natural of studies, while others consider it a corruption and unnatural evil.

Of course, as with all things, the truth lies somewhere in the middle.

Magic, like all other forms of knowledge is more often than not swayed by the user and their individual motivations. Whether it is used for good or evil is usually a reflection of the spell caster rather than the magic itself.

Having lived for far more than my fair share of years, I have encountered many who would abuse magic for their own sinister motives. But I have also had the pleasure of meeting those who have used it for great good.

Mostly though, those whom I have witnessed attempting, succeeding and often failing in the use of magic have been adventurous young people such as yourself.

So go forth and do magic! Take these spells and begin your studies. Perhaps one day you will even achieve the title of Spell Master.

I will watch on with great interest as to your progress, my wonderful 'little witches'.

Young Visitors

I admit to my surprise when three young people turned up at my door asking me to write a book of spells for beginners.

I had thought that any interest in real witch craft had disappeared many decades ago after the horror of the Witch Wars.

Of course, I had heard rumors of the Occult Industry that was thriving, but I have always felt a certain level of disgust for those fraudsters who would make a mockery of witch craft for their own financial gain, so I took no interest in their activities.

It is my experience that such people care little for spell craft, and much for money, with all their made up spells, robes, necklaces, rings and anything else they can possibly deceive the public into purchasing.

Magic rings? What utter nonsense! How is it people are so easily fooled?

But for once these idiots had actually done something of use. They had deceived these youths to the point where they became so angry that they walked away from the commercial mockery and sought out a real witch to learn real witch craft.

And here they were, standing on my doorstep, begging me for spells.

How could I resist?

So here I give you the little book of magic spells for witches, a beginner's course into the world of witch craft. Courtesy of some glorious technology that once would have appeared to be magic itself.

It has been a long time since I have been out into the world, and it seems to have changed much more than I had imagined, but if there really are more people out there who want to know the world of magic, then I am obligated to assist them in that endeavor.

Strangely enough, as it turns out, I don't actually have to go anywhere. I can do it all here in my own home. Oh the joy of computers!

If only it had been this easy back in the old days. But I digress. You are here to learn spells, not listen to an old man ramble.

Take these simplest of spells and use them as you wish. Once you have mastered them, more will quickly follow.

I'm sure that things will turn out just fine. And if not, the world will not end over a few broken hearts and random deaths.

Good luck my "little witches" and I leave you with the smallest of warnings.

"Craft your spells well,
For you reap exactly what you sow".

Spells
Of
Love

Ah Love, the stuff of legend. All have sought it. Few have found it. And many have thought they had it, only to see it slip away between their grasping fingers.

For thousands of years, Witches have crafted spells to find and seize this illusive force. Often without success, and more often with twisted successes that left them wishing they had never sought it in the first place.

But for those brave enough, there are spells that will bring all sorts of love, from the purely physical to the deeply emotional. Use these spells at your own risk, and complain not if they backfire. If your intentions are pure, you will find something of great beauty. Of course, like so many before you, if your intentions are otherwise, you will suffer the consequences.

Good luck young would be lovers. I shall watch with great amusement as to the results of your love spells.

The Spark of Love

This spell is dedicated to turning the heart of another your way. It is intended to create a spark in the mind of that person that will give you a head start toward romance. It is best used by someone who needs some initial aid in getting the attention of the one they would love.

It requires that you obtain either some of their hair or other DNA, such as toe nails or beard etc. Even a finger print will do if you can take a cup or pen that they have used.

1.   Take the item that is from them and place it on a naturally occurring surface. This can be earth, grass, wood, water or any other surface that has not been tampered with chemically.

2.   Be silent and remove all things and problems from your mind. This can take time and requires some patience. But you must be peaceful when the spell is spoken. (Try looking at a pleasant natural landscape or picture of such and thinking about that until all problems and

stress are gone from your life). Gentle music can also be helpful for blocking out the noise of modern day life.

3. Place a small glass of milk next to you. This is the juice of all mothers. It has properties that are essential to magic and good health.

4. Recite the spell once and once only. Speak clearly and at a normal vocal level. Do not shout or whisper. Do not perform while crying, emotionally unstable or angry.

5. Drink half of the milk. This will connect you to all life and engage many magical properties in your history.

6. Spill the other half over the object you have used. This will connect them to you and the spell that you are performing.

7. Repeat this incantation once a week until you feel the person is opening up to you.

Within three days, you should make contact with or stand near the person of your affections. Be open, friendly, easy going and positive. But do not be obsessive. Obsession is negative and will ruin the spell. If possible, engage them in conversation and find out what sort of things they enjoy and try to do these same things together if you can.

You will be amazed at how open the person will become to engaging with you. They will start to develop an interest as the weeks go past, and within a few months will feel an irresistible pull toward you.

Incantation

Remember to recite the following words only once in any single magical session. To repeat more than once in a solitary planetary rotation can have devastating and unfortunate effects. You may practice the words before-hand, but do not include the rest of the ceremony until you are ready to carry it through.

Once the incantation is finished, carry on with the rest of the ceremony and wait for the results. You will soon find that it is much easier to be noticed by this person and they will be far more open to you than they were before. After a while, they will find you quite fascinating.

Make good use of this opportunity, because it may be the only one you get. If you fail to make use of the magic with three days, the spell will be broken.

The Words

Come to me,
My heart's desire

Bring me joy,
With love like fire

Take my heart,
Love it true
Just like I,
Would do to you

True Love

This spell was created to discover if someone will be your true love and stay with you forever. It is an enormously powerful spell that should only be used by those considering marriage or having children with another person.

This spell requires a photograph or drawn image of the person involved. A photograph of you together with that person is especially powerful. This spell can take several hours to perform.

1. Prepare yourself for at least 14 days, drinking only water, tea, natural juices and milk. During this time consume only fruits, vegetables, meat, bread and cereals. Avoid all sugary processed foods, fizzy drinks and corporate foods like McDonalds. Do not smoke, use drugs or consume alcohol. You want to purge any toxins that could have an effect on the outcome of this spell. The healthier you are the more powerful this spell will be.

2.   Sit in a quiet space where you will not be disturbed.
     If you can find somewhere near water, or lie on the
     ground looking at the moon or the clouds, that would
     be especially powerful. But if not, a quiet locked room
     will do. Night time is also good for eliminating the
     noise of modern day society.

3.   Take the photo / picture and place it beside you. It
     can be no more than one arms-length from your body
     and the closer it is the better. If you are able to put
     in on your chest, this is even better.

4.   Think deeply about the person you are considering
     marrying or having children with. Concentrate on their
     good points as well as their bad points. This may take
     an hour or more. Sometimes it will take several hours
     to think about them openly and honestly.

5.   When you are ready and your thoughts of the person
     are honest, uninhibited by emotion, recite the
     incantation seven times.

6.   Continue to think about both their good points and bad
     points. If the spell has worked, one will quickly
     dominate over the other, almost blocking out the other
     view.

7.   If it is their good points that your heart naturally
     moves toward, then they are the love of your life. If
     the images in your head turn to mostly bad,
     problematic or irritating qualities of that person, this is
     not the individual that you are meant to be with.

The effects of this spell are immediate and the answer will
become obvious straight away. It is recommended that if for
any reason this is not the person you will spend your life
with, then you should break up with them as soon as practical.

The reason for this is that after this spell has been
performed, nature will start to send signs against your
relationship with increasing regularity. If you resist nature,
there will be negative consequences to your life. Some of
these can be quite traumatic.

Incantation

Recite this incantation seven times. This is a special number that opens up your mind to the truth. Any less and you will be in denial, any more and the spell will become useless because you will be too sensitive to your emotions.

Within minutes of reciting this spell seven times, your mind will sway one way or the other as Gaea answers your question. Listen to her and then go forward with your life as appropriate. If you fail to listen to her and try to force love on the person, they will turn from you. The more you try to control them, the more bitter they will feel toward you.

This spell can never be broken. If they are the one for you, and you decide not to follow through with them, then you will have lost the opportunity.

The Words

Mother Gaea,
Sacred one

Look ahead,
A thousand suns

Can you help?
To make me see,

Is this my love?
Or should I flee,

A small obsession

A particularly dangerous spell for obvious reasons, this will make a person forget all others and favor you over any. In other words, they will become somewhat obsessed with you. Their feelings of emotional and sexual attracted will be dominantly toward you. But beware, all people dream of being an object of desire, but in reality you might not like that much attention.

You will require an image of the person, or a personal object that belongs to them.

1.   Take the image or object of the individual and place it in clean water. It doesn't matter whether it is a glass of water, a bucket of water, the bath or the shower, just as long as it is not dirty or murky.

2.   Hold the image or object to your chest and keep it as near to your heart as you can.

3.   Masturbate while reciting the incantation repeatedly. Stir or mix your resulting bodily fluids in with the water. Let them run naturally into the water for greater effect.

4.   Repeat each day until that person starts taking a strong interest in you.

This spell will begin to work within days. Sometimes it will only require hours if they already had any interest in you. You should engage the person in conversation. Keep it light and friendly until you see their interest in you starting to grow strong. It will be very obvious.   From there, you can do as you wish. They will have no defenses to your charms whatsoever.

Be very clear that this person will soon have a strong emotional and sexual interest in you and hearts are easily broken.

If you perform this spell on someone that you only have a passing interest in, or discover they are not who you thought they were, you could find it very difficult to get rid of them, and you may even cause a severe reaction on their part.

Many men and women have killed themselves or others after becoming the victim to irresponsible witches who perform this spell without regard to the long term effects. It is not recommended for use by low level witches.

Incantation

Before uttering these words, think carefully about the consequences. There is no going back once you have enchanted an individual to be mildly obsessed with you.

The results can vary enormously based on the personality of the person, their previous association with you and their temperament. It not recommended unless you are absolutely certain that this is the person you wish to spend the rest of your life with and you need assistance in drawing them to you.

The Words

Girls and boys,
More than toys

Let this one,
Be mine

Show their heart,
My gentle face

Then let them come,
With time

Only I,
And no one else

Shall play upon
Their mind

Eyes of Lust

This is a light hearted little spell that many Witches use. It will result in a romantic fling with the individual that it is performed on but will not be strong enough to develop into a long term serious relationship. It is designed for sexual gratification, fun and little more.

You will require an image of the person or one of their small personal possessions. You will also require a glass of milk, one stick of cinnamon and a box of matches.

Little harm will come from this spell as long as it is treated responsibly. So don't go performing it on someone who is married with children (obviously). Just use it for what it was intended for, a romantic tryst.

1.   Go to a quiet place and think of the person you would like to draw to you.

2.   Place the photo or object in a bowl. Place the cinnamon stick on top and spill some milk on them.

Then pick up the cinnamon stick and stir it around in the milk.

3.   Recite the incantation seven times while stirring.

4.   Place the cinnamon stick back on the photo or object.

5.   Light the match and thrust it gently into the milk until the flame goes out.

This spell will work instantly. All you have to do after that is engage the person in conversation and suggest that you spend time together, whether it is going out for a drink or a meal, or watching a movie. It really doesn't matter. They will be swayed toward a sexual relationship with you no matter what the situation.

This spell is likely to result in a lot of fun for you and your chosen recipient.

Incantation

Recite the following words while stirring the cinnamon stick in the juice of the mother (milk). This will bring a spicy quality to your life in the form of exciting sexual escapades. The milk will open up your recipient to magic, and the cinnamon will stir their inner desire for you, while adding flavoring to that desire.

The effects of this spell are instant. If it is successfully carried out, the recipient will be putty in your hands for the next few months.

The Words

Heart of fire,
Mind of desire

Your hands will soften,
And touch me often

Pleasures done,
Consequences none

Lots of fun,
Under the sun

Come to me,
Mine you will be

The Envy of others

This is a more complex spell that will make many people love you and change your life to one that others will envy you for. It can take up to a year or more to prepare for and will leave you in a state of fitness and health that will last a life time, partly due to conditioning and partly due to magic.

This one is only for the more serious and dedicated Witch who is committed to leading the best life they can and being very successful throughout that life.

1. You will need to take up an exercise regime that you will stick to and change your diet to an extremely healthy balanced intake of food. You goal is to get into very good shape before committing this spell. Preferably you want to end up with less than 3% body fat. You will also need to be free of all the toxins of modern day life. For this, you should consume only natural foods such as meat, vegetables, fruits, cereals and breads. You should drink only water, milk and tea.

2. Continue this regime for one full rotation of the earth around the sun. If you are not slim and fit by that stage, then do a second rotation and work harder to lose weight and tone your muscles.

3. When you feel ready you will need to go to a secluded place amongst nature. Parks and fields are by far the best option as you will need to be able to see the moon.

4. Lie on the ground and focus on your breathing until you are completely relaxed.

5. Recite the incantation three times.

6. Lie there for at least one more hour to give the moon a chance to receive your message and bond with you.

The effects of this spell are immediate, and from that point on the moon will influence your body, helping to create the perfect balance between all your bodily systems, maintaining good health and allowing you to live an extraordinary life. You will find it easier to stay in shape, your level of success will improve and opportunities will start to flow your way much faster and more often until they are flooding in.

You will look younger and feel younger for the simple reason that your body will BE younger. The spell will undo much of the damage (aging) that a poor lifestyle has had on you, literally making you younger in the process. Even your organs will function better allowing you to live longer.

You will become capable of achieving anything you put your mind too, and people will be almost falling over them-selves to help you do it.

You will be the envy of people's eyes.

Incantation

Recite these words to yourself. Use whatever level of voice you like but just make sure you are talking to yourself. You must be the absolute focus of the spell. Your only thoughts should be on the body, fitness and lifestyle that you want for yourself. Forget everything and everybody else. They don't matter anymore.

Once you have recited this three times, remember to lie there for at least an hour. The moon needs to bond with you and match your life's rhythm. Once that is done, you will feel a much stronger connection to nature and things will start going very well for you.

The Words

Into me
Spirits enter

Let me be
The only Center

Let all others look
Upon me with lust

And my body and soul
Make it just

I would seek
All I can

For one life only
Is my span

Desire

All people wish to be desired. It is a natural human emotion. But very few end up achieving it and even fewer end up enjoying it. But for any who wish to be in such a position, there is a curious little spell that originated in the fifth century BC in what is now Amesbury, Wiltshire, Southern England.

This spell will allow you to appear far more impressive to the world by enhancing all your best attributes and eliminating bad ones. This will create an aura that others can sense but not see. It will make you attractive to others and make them want to like you.

You will require only a cauliflower blended into a juice, a mirror and a small bowl of milk, plus a face cloth for the milk.

Preparation

Before using this spell, you need to purify yourself for fourteen days. Consume only vegetable juice for the fourteen days. This will provide the necessary micro nutrients for cellular transformation and purge your body of most of the toxins of modern day life.

1. Find a private place with a mirror.

2. Place the face cloth in the milk to soak.

3. Recite part one of the spell.

4. Wash your face with the milk, and leave the residue on your face for the duration of the spell.

5. Drink the cauliflower juice. Its magical properties will begin the process of cellular transformation. Curiously enough, cauliflower will also protect you from most cancers (which is really just poisoning by another name) if you consume it regularly.

6. Recite part two of the spell.

7. Wash the milk residue from your face.

The spell will take effect over the following fourteen days, in which it is essential that you continue to avoid toxins and provide micro nutrients by consuming only vegetable juice.

From there, it will be up to you to decide how you use it. People will start looking on you with newfound respect and opportunities will begin to come your way. You will find it easier to learn new skills and talents and you will also become smarter. If you start to eat a well-balanced diet and exercise daily, you will find that the spell will enhance these to dramatic levels. This can be the start of an incredible life.

Incantation

This is a very simple spell, yet the results can be very far reaching. Some people have gone on to become famous actors, models and multi-millionaires. For such a tiny spell, the results are extremely positive.

The effects of this spell will occur over the following fourteen days if you maintain your micro nutrients and keep toxins from your body. You will experience an actual physical transformation, far in excess of what would occur through normal exercise and healthy eating.

The Words

Part One

Take this body
Make it right

Remove the flaws
From my sight

Give me the life
That I deserve

From me hold nothing
In reserve

Part Two

Do it now
Make it right

Change my life
On this night

The Match Maker

This is an unusual spell that involves two third parties rather than the spell caster. It allows a Witch to influence two others into a relationship. It is supposed to be used for kindness, but is often misused by those seeking financial reward for their services.

If performed well, it can lead your friends to wonderful loving relationships. But when misused, it can have all sorts of terrible consequences.

You will require extremely personal items from both parties. Preferably their blood, but if this is unavailable, then something they wear regularly will have to suffice. But blood really is far better.

1.   Take the blood or personal items and place them together in a hole in the ground. Cover them with dirt and leave them there. This will help bond both spirits to the earth.

2. Write out the names of both people on the same piece of paper and place it over the mound where you buried the blood/items. This will now help bond the spirits together as well.

3. Recite the first part of the incantation. This creates the bond previously mentioned.

4. Light a match and burn the piece of paper until there is nothing left but ashes. This symbolizes that they are meant to be together until the end.

5. Recite the second part of the incantation. This will create a link between the two physical people.

6. Pour milk over the ashes. This will allow magic to take hold.

The results will always vary. If you performed the spell for good reasons, then it is likely that both parties will appreciate it. If you did it for money, chances are the party that paid you has some very nasty surprises to unleash.

After the spell is completed, you should take the time to introduce the two parties to each other. If the spell worked, that is all that will be required. They will naturally take it further from there.

Incantation

Think carefully before carrying this spell out. Do those two people REALLY belong together? If so, then perform the spell as required and feel satisfied that you have added some love (and undoubtedly lust) to the world.

It's a simple spell, but usually very effective.

The Words

Part One

Let two become one
And one become two

Each other's love
That shall do

Part Two

Let introduction
Turn to love

They shall fly together
Like a pair of doves

Lustful Thoughts

This is one of the less commonly used spells in the modern day, although it was extremely popular in the past. Groups of young people would cast it, and enjoy a night of untamed lust and adventure. The spell literally brings the spell casters fantasies to life.

There are no known side effects to this, as all traces of the spell disappear on the third midnight after the casting, and it dissipates in power drastically after the first night. You must be isolated away from the rest of society to make it last the full three days and nights. Otherwise, reality quickly interferes with the magic involved.

It requires an area that is preferably isolated, or at least locked off to the outside world. It also requires a willing group of fifteen people and five large bottles of apple cider.

1.   In a room, sit your participants in a circle with a hexagram drawn between them. There should be a

female at each of the five points of the hexagram, and two people in the circle between each point person.

2. The female at the head of the hexagram should recite the first part of the incantation then drink a mouthful from the cider. She should then pass it around the circle, giving each member a drink until the bottle has returned to her. She then drinks what is left.

3. Next the whole group recites the second part of the incantation together.

4. The point female to the left of her will then do the same, reciting the first part of the incantation, drinking a mouthful of cider and passing it on till it returns to her to finish off.

5. The group once again recites the second part of the incantation together.

6. Carry on this process until all five points have taken their turn and the cider has been fully consumed.

7.   The first female will once again repeat the first part of the incantation, followed by the group repeating the second.

From there, go about your night as you would and events will quickly start to turn to fantasy as magic takes hold. People will find they are able to think of things they never knew before, talk about mystical subjects and see things they can't normally see. Many will be overcome with lust as their true desires for each other emerge. Some participants may even experience shape shifting of their bodies.

This is low level magic at its best.

Incantation

This spell is essentially harmless. It is designed to bring fantasies to life. It has been often used in the past, but dropped out of favor in the modern world due to people's ridiculous focus on money instead of enjoying their life.

Although occasionally there have been cases where the fantasy has got out of hand, the limited time frame to this spell makes it hard for anything truly bad to take hold. All effects tend to disappear within the space of three midnights passing.

The effects of this spell begin at midnight the following day. From that point on, there is little that cannot occur. You will find yourself engaging in activities that were previously restricted to your fantasies.

The Words

Part One

Ashes to ashes
Dust to dust

Let these lovers
Be joined in lust

Wealth, Sex,
And fun abound

All their desires
Will come around

Part Two

Let them succumb
To wonderful pleasures

To return again
At their leisure

Spells
Of
Wealth

Wealth is such a funny thing. Most people do not even know what it is, let alone what to do with it, throwing away their opportunities on silly distractions and trivial purchases.

But for those witches who do understand the difference between money, currency and actual wealth, there are almost endless amounts to be had.

The first five made it so.

Having suffered so bitterly themselves they decided that others should not have to go through such hardship and created a portal for wealth to flow to you in vast sums.

This was the most powerful spell ever cast and is built into the very fabric of reality itself. It provides a way that all Witches can go about their lives without the worry of hunger and destitution.

Think wisely on these spells and the advice of those spell casters who were more powerful than you will ever be, for it will decide not only your income, but your very future.

If you follow their wise words, you will find that life can be very rich indeed. Wealth will flow to you, pouring like a never ending waterfall into your life.

But if you are overcome with greed or just too lazy and arrogant to do as instructed, then you will end up like so many others, wondering where your next meal will come from.....

I and many others shall watch with great interest as to who gets it right, and who gets it wrong.

A Gift of Wealth

This spell is for immediate financial aid. It will seek out the wealth around you and send a little bit your way to get you through. It is not a long term solution, but will help you in that moment of greatest need.

You will require a piece of paper, a pen, a glass of milk and a mint.

1.   Find a quiet place to sit and be alone. It should be quiet enough to let you focus, and not be distracted by the sounds of modern day life.

2.   Write your name on the piece of paper. Then fold it in half. This is telling nature that you only have part of what you require.

3.   Recite the first part of the incantation.

4. Place the piece of paper in the milk. It will allow magic to take its course along the path of the spell you have begun.

5. Place the mint in your mouth.

6. Drink the glass of milk.

7. Take the mint out of your mouth and place it in the glass.

8. Recite the second part of the incantation.

This spell will give you some breathing space and prevent you from starving. But it is highly recommended to follow it up with the magic wealth plan that you will find at the end of this section. That will guarantee you lifelong wealth that will prevent such events reoccurring.

This particular spell can only be used once by any Witch, so use it wisely.

Incantation

Recite these words clearly. Speak them only once and do not shout. The spell is passive, not aggressive, and force can ruin the incantation. As stated, this spell can only be used once.

At midnight, the spell shall take effect and a small amount of wealth shall come to you in the following days that will allow you to carry on. But remember your promise! You must make all efforts to improve your life and financial situation. If you waste the money that comes to you, or continue on a wasteful path, then you will face far worse situations in days to come.

The Words

Part One

My hands are tired
My stomach rumbles

Help me now
For I have stumbled

Give this poor soul
A decent meal

I do not wish
To have to steal

Part Two

Give to me
Enough to live

In return
I promise to give

My earnest efforts
To change my ways

And make better use
Of future days

A life of splendor

Naturally many witches have found themselves without funds due to a failure to understand the basic mathematics of wealth. This spell has allowed them to undo much of the damage and get back on the right track.

It requires a piece of paper, a pen, a calculator, your last pay slip, a mint leaf, a glass of milk and a willingness to change your ways once you have the assistance of magic.

1. Find a nice pleasant place to sit and clear your mind. Think about all the nice things you would like to have in your life. Your dream home, travel, a nice car etc...

2. Place the mint leaf in the glass of milk.

3. Recite the first part of the spell.

4. Write your name on the piece of paper.

5. Use your pay slip and the calculator to see exactly how much money you take home after taxes in a month. Write that figure under your name on the paper.

6. Times that figure by twelve to find out how much you make in a year after taxes. Write that figure underneath the last.

7. Times that figure by the number of years you have till you are sixty years old. Write that figure below the last.

8. Look at that figure and think about it. That is how much you are going to earn throughout the rest of your working life if you do not change your ways.

9. Drink the milk.

10. Now times that final figure by five and write it above your name.

11.   Fold the paper up and keep it in your wallet for the rest of your life.

12.   Recite the second part of the spell

The spell is complete. If you keep the paper and begin to follow the Witches Right at the end of this section, nature will help you achieve the last figure you wrote. But if you throw it away or don't follow the formula, you will find that you only earn the figure in step 7.

Incantation

Repeat these words only once, and like all wealth spells, it can only be used once by any witch. So don't waste it.

The effects of this spell are immediate, but are affected greatly by your own attitude. You will quickly find that the more responsibility that you take with your budget, the more money shall flow to you. For every dollar that you save, five more dollars shall come.

If you stick with it, you will achieve the final figure you wrote of five times your life's income.

The Words

Part One

Twists and turns
My money burns

Foolish me
Poor to be

It runs from me each single day
The cash in my pocket flies away

Part Two

Help me change
I want to know

Just how far
My money can go

Show me how
To make ends meet

And ensure forever
That I shall eat

Money, Money, Everywhere

This spell was created over the centuries by those who would have more gold. Many had little idea of how to grow their wealth and did not really understand the entire concept of building their fortunes. So a few of them decided to create some short cuts to the financial security they dreamed of.

This was one of the few spells that seemed to bring the rain of Gold that they all desired.

You will require one solid gold or solid silver coin. It must be gold or silver, because this is real money.

*Paper money is a worthless scam perpetrated on a stupid public to steal their wealth without giving anything in return (curiously enough, the result of another spell cast in the 18th century by some very nasty people).

1. Make sure that you are in a quiet and secure place. You don't want to go down in history for being the Witch that got robbed.

2. Make a list of things that are important to you, but that you cannot afford. Things such as a mortgage free home, travel overseas etc.

3. Lie on your back and place the coin on your forehead. This will begin to put wealth into your mind.

4. Recite the incantation once. This will connect you, magic and wealth.

5. Start to think of all the things that you would like to have, but cannot currently afford to have. This will connect you, magic, wealth and your dreams.

6. Read your list out loud. Now nature will know exactly what you want.

7. Recite the incantation again.

8.   Read the list again.

9.   Do this until you have recited the incantation and read your list five times, so that all of the first five will hear you.

10. Stand up without removing the coin.

11. Now take the coin out of your mouth.

The effects of this spell will occur relatively quickly. You will start to find that you have more opportunities for making money, as well as more ways toward some of the items on your list. Within a month, your finances should have improved considerably.

Now follow this up by reading the Witches Right and obeying it to the letter. If you do so, you will find that you will never go without money again.

Incantation

Speak these words clearly and loudly. You don't have to shout, but don't whisper either. Make sure the coin never leaves your head during this ceremony.

This is a reasonably powerful spell, because it taps into the greatest spell that was ever cast by the First Five. You will notice its effects very quickly as things start to turn around for you financially. This must be matched by your own deeds. Otherwise, you will learn the price of the term, "easy come, easy go", the hard way.

Use this as your opportunity to change and the financial benefits will just keep flowing your way.

The Words

Come to me
Seek me out

Turn my fortunes
Inside out

Gold and Silver
Provide protection

Against that evil
Hungry reflection

Let things be
How they should

Let me live
How I would

The Witches Right

This is not a spell, but a specially crafted budget that contains much magic and is built into the very foundations of nature here on earth. It was created in the earliest days of Witchery at the very first meeting of Witches where all five of the participants found themselves with little if any assets and no gold to speak of. Deciding that their situation was mainly due to injustice, they created a solution for themselves and all who would come after them.

As a result, they created a spell of enormous power that changed the very fabric of reality itself. It is the most powerful spell ever created and cannot be undone, because it is based on Gold, the most powerful of all the elements. It was put in place to protect Witches from the hunger that consumes so many others.

To any who follow this formula, you will find that the returns become enormous over time. In fact, for every piece of gold or silver that you save, five more will come your way.

This is the Witches Right.

1. Divide all the gold and silver that you earn into ten equal parts.

2. The first part is your own, yours to save for the purchase of real wealth such as land, crops and businesses, all those things that will always have value and bring you both security and income in their own right. For each coin you put to this purpose will come five more as gifts.

3. The second part is for the King, to keep his sword in its sheath. Hide what you have too, but give him no more than one part, as his lust for the wealth of others is never ending. For these coins, you will receive no replacement, but will keep your head, a fair bargain by any standard.

4. The third part is for your old age. For one day you will no longer be able to earn, but you will still need to eat. Find a safe place and keep this money for when

that day comes. And when it does arrive, you will find that for every coin you gave, five more have mysteriously appeared.

5.   The other seven parts will carry you through your daily life, paying for all that you must have, all that you must pay for, and a few of the things that you desire. But for any who spend more than seven parts, there will come a day when they starve, wither and die.

6.   For any who are wise enough to spend less than seven parts, each extra coin you save will be returned with another five over time.

7.   If this is done, then you shall never go hungry and you shall end up with all that you desire, more powerful than a King and far wealthier than the money lenders.

Many Witches have followed this advice and gone on to live very comfortable lives. Many have not and have ended up in poverty. All Witches are advised to make use of this most powerful spell and go on to live without hunger and hardship as the First Five intended them too.

Spells
Of
Harm

It is often the nature of men to wish each other harm. Sometimes with just reason, but most times out of greed and jealousy toward those they would maim or kill.

I have little interest in helping the unjust, but plenty of interest in helping those who are decent and downtrodden to gain their terrible revenge on those who are not.

So here we have a few nasty little spells to bring such vengeance to all those who have maligned you. Whether it is the wonderful little bundle of joy known as the spell of irritation, or the slightly more serious spell of death, all of these spells tend to work extremely well.

Some I have used, and others I have had recommended to me. I'm sure you will enjoy them. For each will make the world a better place when cast upon men of an evil nature.

Good luck, and remember, most people have got death coming to them. All you're doing is speeding things up.

Spell of Irritation

This spell is designed to cause irritation to the life of someone who has done you wrong, or harmed you. It will make things more difficult for them and cause many of their achievements to go haywire. They will think that they have succeeded, only to be greatly disappointed soon after. It will begin to seem as if nothing in their lives can possibly go right.

You will require a personal item of the person you are wishing to get back at. The more personal the item is the better. So a watch, pair of shoes, school bag, favorite pen or something else that they use every day would be perfect. You will also need some milk, some dirt and a bottle of water.

1.   Take the item that is from them and place it on a naturally occurring surface. This can be earth, grass, wood, water or any other surface that has not been tampered with chemically.

2.   Spill some milk over the object to open it up to the magic of the World. Let it sit for an hour to allow the

milk to begin to go off. This is how you will twist their lives. Everything they do will spoil as well

3.   Recite the incantation three times, throwing a small amount of dirt on the object after each recital. This is what will bury the person in misery.

4.   Dispose of the object thoroughly and secretly. Nobody else must know what happened to it in order to prevent the spell being reversed. You can incinerate it or bury it.

5.   Drink the entire bottle of water, to purify yourself of any dark secretions.

The effects of this spell will usually last about a year or so. It can be repeated if necessary. From the following day, the recipient will start to have ever increasingly bad luck.

Nothing serious will happen to them, but nothing will go quite the way they want it too either.

Incantation

This incantation is to be repeated three times, with dirt used in between each recital as per the spell.

The results of this spell will begin the following day after dawn. It will start with little things and eventually build to the point where everything seems to go wrong for the recipient. They will spend a year unable to achieve any of the things they want without it going sour.

The spell will last through one full rotation of the planet around the sun.

The Words

Hear me mother,
Let justice come

A terrible wrong,
Has been done

Seek my enemy
On the changing hour

Teach them the lesson,
That all things can sour

Spell of Misfortune

This is a more serious spell that will bring very bad things to the person it is cast upon. It is intended for use against people who have significantly harmed you, as the effects can be extremely serious both physically and mentally.

It is not to be used in a trivial manner, or against those who have merely slighted you. The most common use of this spell is against rapists, local thugs and murderers.

You will require the ability to throw or place a stone into the yard or accommodation building of the person you are casting it on. As such you will require a small rock or stone (stone is better). You will also need paper, pen and a box of matches.

1. Go to an isolated quiet spot where you will not be disturbed. Make it a place the recipient is unlikely to have ever been.

2. Recite the incantation once. This will begin the spell.

3. Write the person's name on the piece of paper by hand. This is the beginning of binding them to the spell that you just recited.

4. Place the paper on the ground and hold it down with the rock/stone. But leave their name uncovered. This symbolizes holding the recipient down.

5. Recite the words of the incantation three more times. This will tie them to it without doubt and prevent the spell being undone.

6. Light a match and burn the paper thoroughly. It may take several matches to do this, but all of the letters of their name should be burnt. This part is very important.

7. Take the stone and go to the person's home and cast it into their yard. If they do not have a yard, then choose an area that they will pass by regularly, such as a workplace or corridor of an apartment building that

they frequent. If you can place it outside their front door, or somewhere they often stand, this will be especially powerful.   But it is important that they will go there within the next three days after the spell is cast.

Incantation

Speak the words clearly and confidently. Do not whisper or shout as this can change the effect of the spell, and ruin its ability to harm the recipient.

This spell will take effect within a month and the recipient will begin to have serious problems in their lives. It is not uncommon for them to end up in prison, or even be killed within one rotation of the planet around the sun. It all depends on how evil they are, as this spell essentially sends their own nastiness back at them.

88

The Words

Terrible anger,
Inside I feel

Naked revenge,
Will be my meal

Go to the person,
Who treated me wrong

Ruin their lives,
Let their misery be long

The Spell of Death

One of the more serious of the harmful spells, this will bring inevitable death to anyone you cast it on. Often that death will be drawn out and miserable, either through bad health or injury. However, sometimes if their inner evil is more extreme, the death will come quickly and violently.

It is only to be used on the absolute worst of people such as murderers, rapists, burglars, robbers and thieves.

You will require a piece of paper, a pen, a sharp knife, some malt vinegar and a glass or bottle of water.

1. Find a quiet isolated spot to perform your ritual. It is important that you will not be disturbed, as you are dealing in very powerful magic and none should know that you are responsible.

2. Relax yourself. Calm your mind of any stress you may feel so that the spell will be concentrated.

3.   Read the first incantation. This will begin the magic.

4.   Pour about a table spoon or two of the vinegar into the water and let it mix naturally. Do not stir it. Nature is combining magic with reality and bitterness with life.

5.   While it is mixing, write the name of the person onto the piece of paper so that nature shall know the person who shall suffer.

6.   Recite the second incantation. This will tie the person to your spell and bind them to their death.

7.   Drink about half of the vinegar water. Then pour the other half on the piece of paper. Your bitterness toward them will now be the cause of their downfall.

8.   Recite the third incantation.

9.   Take the knife and stab the paper repeatedly. This will separate them from their life.

The effects of this spell are often mixed. Sometimes the person will die in days, other times they will develop a disease and die miserably over several years. But either way, they will die. Be warned though, that if nature finds they were not bad people and did nothing to deserve such a fate, it will instead deliver that fate upon the spell binder.

Incantation

This spell will invoke magic that originated in England with the first tribes. Their spirits that still watch over the land shall deliver a bitter fate to the recipient. Once invoked, it is best to forget about it and let the darkness do its job. One day in the near future, you will undoubtedly hear that the person is dead or dying.

This spell cannot be revoked. Once cast, there is no going back.

The Words

Part One

Darkest beings,
In all of time

Hear me now,
Make my rhyme

Part Two

See this person
Bind them true

To the spell
I cast to you

Part Three

Let this persons,
End come swift

To them from me,
A parting gift

Death comes easy

This is a curious little spell that will increase the chance of death to someone who has wronged you. It will not guarantee that they will die, but will certainly make them more susceptible to death whenever they do anything stupid or foolish. So the death will still be completely their own fault, but you just helped them along a little bit. That makes you a very helpful person.

This spell is usually used against people who are just plain nasty. Whether it be the horrible bureaucratic office manager who humiliates you, the obnoxious landlord who rips you off or the bully who picks on you. They all deserve what is coming to them in the end. You're just increasing their chances of it happening sooner rather than later.

It requires an image of the person, whether it be a photo or a drawing. It also requires a bucket of water to submerge the image in and a glass of milk.

1. Take the image and submerge it in the bucket of water for three days leading up to a full moon.

2. For that same three days, you must consume only natural foods, such as meat, vegetables, fruit, bread and cereal. Drink only natural drinks such as juices, milk, tea and water. Do not consume alcohol, drugs, fizzy drinks or cigarettes.

3. On the third day, kneel over the bucket of water and pour a glass of milk into it. Let it mix naturally and do not stir.

4. Recite the incantation.

5. Take the bucket outside and tip it into dirt, grass or a garden.

The effects of this spell are immediate from the moment the bucket spills on the earth, and that person shall start to become far more susceptible to danger and death.

Incantation

Recite the words as you look into the contents of the bucket.

This spell will take a while to work. Once the full moon has passed, it will take one more month till the next full moon for the spell to be completed.

Then the recipient will suddenly find themselves on deaths door, always ready to step over the threshold.

The Words

Take this image
Let the word go out

To them any
May bring death about

Let this liquid
Symbolize their blood

To be spilled by all
Like a flood

Make death come easy
To this fool

Soon they will sink
In sweet deaths pool

So now we have reached the end of this wonderful little book. Have you gained any wisdom? Have you tried any spells?

I hope you have, because that is the only way to learn.

Perhaps some spells worked and perhaps some failed, but take some advice from a very, very old man. Practice makes perfect, especially when it comes to the crafting of magic.

So keep at it. Perfect your craft and learn all that you can from it. That is the only way you will get anywhere in life, no matter what you do. Nobody is born an expert at anything, and even the most powerful Spell Masters take many decades to learn their craft. And take heart that you are probably a better witch than I was when I first started all those years ago.

I shall follow your progress with great amusement, and when enough of you are ready I shall send you something more advanced to learn.

In the meantime, there are certainly many things that you can do to make yourself a better witch.

Live Naturally

This is an important aspect of any witches life, for you cannot seek contact with nature if you are not part of nature yourself. Any witch worthy of their spell book spends much time in the fresh air, amongst the plants and near the water.

They walk, they run, they grow a garden. They feed the birds and own a pet. They bask in the sun and let the rain fall on their face. For all such things will bring appreciation of nature.

So, what can you do personally to improve your spell casting? Park the car and walk. Leave the city and live somewhere you can have a garden. Throw out the fizzy drinks and partake in water and milk. Get off the sofa and go for a run. Do all the things that will make your stronger, and be rid of all things that weaken you.

The closer you are to nature, the more success you will have with your spells.

Think on such things. Then act on them.

Lightning Source UK Ltd.
Milton Keynes UK
UKHW02f1935151117
312811UK00006B/327/P